# The Falkirk Wheel

## Art and Engineering by **RMJM**

# Introduction

The Falkirk Wheel is a revolutionary boat lift which connects the Union Canal with the Forth and Clyde Canal. It is the focal point of the Millennium Link – Britain's most ambitious ever canal restoration project which has seen £78 million invested in linking the east and west coasts of Scotland via a refurbished inland waterway.

The Wheel itself was designed by Tony Kettle of UK-based international architects RMJM as part of a multi-skilled team acting on behalf of British Waterways. It now forms the centre piece of this historic link – stretching from Glasgow to Edinburgh – and as such, it always had to be much more than a boat lift. It had to be a celebration of what had been achieved, a monument to the Millennium, a symbol for Scotland in the 21st century. It had to join two canals. It had to unite two historic cities and it had to merge art and engineering together in one powerful statement.

On the following pages, we will look at how this was achieved. We will consider the geographical and historical context. We will look at the creative process and how RMJM-led design innovation runs throughout the project from conception to the final engineering solution. We will briefly explore the landscape of art and engineering to discover what the Wheel has to say about both and about Scotland at the dawn of the new Millennium.

# The Falkirk Wheel

## A personal perspective

# Preface

Her Majesty The Queen with James M Stirling, Director of British Waterways Scotland inaugurating the Falkirk Wheel in May 2002

When I first heard about this project it was clear that this was something with the potential to make a real cultural statement. It was symbolic; this physical reconnecting of east and west Scotland, Glasgow and Edinburgh, the Forth and Clyde Canal with the Union Canal.

Our solution to the physical connection, developed from first principles, is the first rotating boat lift ever built and the first boat lift to be built in Britain since the Anderson boat lift in 1895. All sorts of options had been considered, both by others and within RMJM, but the fundamental idea was simple: lift the boats up 35 metres from one canal to the other and vice versa.

The starting point for our concept was this linear route or spine that connects the two sides of Scotland. Victorian aqueducts are very thin and elegant and we wanted the one that fed the lift to be equally elegant, but in a modern idiom – a beautiful, organic flowing thing, like the spine of a fish.

However, at the point where it breaks and makes the connection between the two canals, we strongly felt it should be something of a celebration, a statement. So from the outset we were driven both by the aesthetic and practical requirements of the project. This is something that drives us on many projects – not just the Wheel – but also on projects such as Palm Island, Doncaster Racecourse and Experience Northumberland where we are also attempting to express more than basic function.

With the Wheel, we always wanted that expression to be sculptural. We wanted something that would give a sense of movement and rotation, and, of course, this is the function of the hooked leading edges in our final design. But our Wheel also has some of the enduring qualities of a timepiece – precision engineering and intrinsic beauty, metal curves and movement in one composition.

And then there's another dimension. When the Wheel moves, when it turns, something truly special happens. The curves and the water and the reflections – I can only describe it as kaleidoscopic. It is mesmerizing. It blurs any distinction between art and engineering.

Tony Kettle

RMJM

December 2002

two elements
air and water
interact

each meeting
on the plane
of most resistance

air takes water
lifts it tosses it
like dice

throws it
to a height
of sixty feet

makes clouds
that glide
across the surface

of this water
which in turn
takes air

rides with it
impetuous to move
make waves

to travel forward
impelled upon
the instance

by this air
its movement
in complete control

two elements
balletic in response
they dance

entwine
their several beings
interact

**Arabesque by Brian Johnstone**

# Contents

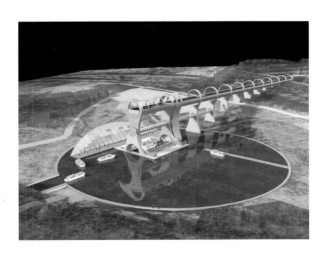

# Celebration

## The Millennium Link

The Falkirk Wheel was designed to reconnect the Forth and Clyde Canal with the Union Canal lying some 35 metres below. It is the focal point of the Millennium Link – a £78 million project which has created a fully navigable waterway between Edinburgh and Glasgow for the first time in almost 70 years.

In addition to the construction of the £17.3 million Wheel (including tunnel, aqueduct, and basin), the Millennium Link project also involved the removal of 32 obstructions to navigation, the building of 28 new road bridges and the diversion of the M8. The momentum behind this ambitious project was provided by a belief that the development of the Millennium Link would create enormous economic and leisure potential. Indeed, experts estimated that the project could assist in creating over 4,000 new full-time jobs across central Scotland.

In the past, the two historic canals had been connected at Falkirk by a staircase of 11 locks which dropped the canal 35 metres over a distance of 1.5 kilometres. The locks were dismantled in 1933 – closing the only navigable link between the two canals. Following subsequent road developments, the Forth and Clyde Canal which was opened in 1790 was finally closed in 1963, while the Union Canal, which opened when the Falkirk locks were built in 1822, was closed in 1965.

The Millennium Link is the biggest engineering project ever undertaken in Scotland by British Waterways – and at its heart is the Falkirk Wheel. Situated in a natural amphitheatre on the west side of Falkirk near Tamfourhill, this revolutionary boat lift massively reduces the time taken to transfer boats from one canal to the other compared with a set of traditional locks.

However, as well as the 35 metre high Wheel, the project to connect the Forth and Clyde and the Union Canals consisted of a further five elements: an extension to the Union Canal; a tunnel beneath the Antonine Wall; a 100 metre wide circular basin at the foot of the boat lift; an aqueduct to connect the Wheel with the Forth and Clyde Canal; and a lock connection to the Forth and Clyde Canal. In addition, there was a need to design and build the visitor centre which now provides dramatic views of the Falkirk Wheel in action.

Completed ahead of schedule in April 2002 and opened in May 2002 by Her Majesty Queen Elizabeth II, the Falkirk Wheel honours the bold vision and imagination behind the Millennium Link itself. It is a functional sculpture which both symbolises and celebrates the renaissance of the two canals – and what may yet follow.

# Foundation

## The RMJM philosophy

RMJM is a design-led leader among UK-based architectural firms with international operations and projects that confirm its ranking among the world's top 20 such professional practices.

As the architects for the Falkirk Wheel and Visitor Centre, RMJM was part of the design and build team asked by British Waterways to present alternatives to the exemplar design which had formed the brief for the project tender.

RMJM's founding modernist credentials were widely acclaimed as long as half a century ago. These credentials are matched today by the creativity of the young team of professionals who spearhead its design and project-focused approach. It is a team dedicated to a philosophy of creating 'an engineered aesthetic' with results that have been described as 'transcending, rather than following, fashion'.

**Doncaster Racecourse**

The Falkirk Wheel is not the only RMJM project to combine art and engineering together in a dramatic statement.

Doncaster Racecourse hosts the St. Leger – the UK's oldest classic race. The new RMJM masterplan for the racecourse looks to remodel and unite a series of isolated buildings of inferior quality to create a new identity for spectators and a worldclass horseracing environment. The identity is changed by unlocking the underlying potential of the site and creating an amphitheatrical form made from a series of overlapping organic forms. The concept is derived from an anatomical drawing by Leonardo Da Vinci of the rear leg of a horse. The metaphor of the separate bones overlaid by muscle and joined by soft ligament is used to inform the overcladding of the orthogonal blocks with an organic skin and the joining of the separate blocks with flexible canvas. These canvas elements provide entrance canopies to the various racecourse enclosures and are able to take up the complicated geometries inherited from the original building layout.

The William Gates building, Cambridge

The pre-eminence of RMJM's design ethos is complemented by a project-orientated and, where appropriate, multi-skilled approach. True teamwork among complementary professional disciplines readily translates into a constructive project partnership with clients and other consultants.

The success of this approach – the combination of an engineered (or process-driven) aesthetic and a multi-skilled capability – can be seen not only in the Falkirk Wheel, but in high profile projects in Asia and the Middle East as well as across the United Kingdom.

**Palm Island**

Palm Island is one of the world's largest manmade islands currently being constructed in Dubai, UAE. The concept developed was based on the palm – and the idea that there should be a single central interchange for boat users which would create a dramatic theatrical amphitheatre. The result is a remarkable building which will create a centrepiece for the island and celebrate the magnitude of the Palm Island concept. The design is derived from the Nymphea or Water Lily, a large beautiful flower sitting in a reflective pool. This metaphor is used to inform the design of shading elements, which radiate from a central opening dome structure. Below the shading elements is a geometric layout of buildings derived from a simple Islamic decorative motif of rotated squares. The organic elements provide shade to the functional orthogonal building forms.

# Re-inventing the brief

The functional brief for the Falkirk Wheel was to take two boats up and take two boats down the 35 metre vertical drop in 15 minutes. It should be remembered, however, that 35 metres is the height of a nine storey building and four boats plus water is equivalent to 600 tonnes!

Previous design ideas – see 'Early Designs' box – were based on four enclosed caissons, each carrying one boat. The caissons were in sets of two, hung from pinned connections at the head with the horizontality of the water and the caissons maintained by gravity. The drive mechanism was a series of hydraulic motors rotating the hub in the centre of the wheel. This was later developed into a rim drive solution, where the Ferris wheel sat directly on the drive mechanism rather than on legs as shown (see image).

The design brief for the design and build contract (eventually won by the Joint Venture Team of Morrison Construction/Bachy Soletanche) was based on the Ferris wheel-type design solution – the same solution that had been used by British Waterways to gain preliminary approvals and raise financial support.

However, as part of the new design and build team, RMJM rejected all the design solutions that had been considered previously (see box). Our challenge was to come up with an alternative form that would be truly worthy for Scotland in the 21st century. Arguably, the most important thing that we brought to the table was an understanding of the massive symbolic and artistic potential of such an important Millennium project. This understanding would be reflected in the way in which RMJM re-invented the brief and re-interpreted the wheel form to create something unique and truly memorable.

**Early Designs**

British Waterways first raised the idea of a boat lift to reconnect the two canals in 1994 – although the first concepts for a rotating boat lift in Europe date back to the 19th century – when it invited Dundee architects, Nicoll Russell Studios, to present designs for a boat lift at Falkirk. The Nicoll Russell concept – a Ferris wheel-type solution – was subsequently used to secure Millennium Commission funding for the project.

British Waterways then opted to proceed down the design and build route and appointed Binnie Black and Veatch as client agent. BB&V came up with an exemplar design resembling the Ferris wheel (see illustration) which formed the brief for the project tender. When the Morrison/Bachy Soletanche consortium, which had been working with RMJM, successfully secured the tender, RMJM set out to re-appraise the design of the 'wheel' from first principles.

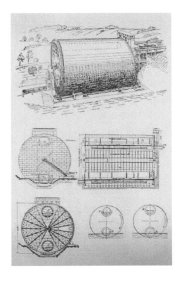 

# Inspiration

## Design and rationale

When asked by British Waterways to come up with alternatives to the exemplar design and build tender design, we held an internal design competition between three RMJM directors and their teams. Each group worked up independent proposals and then gathered together to brainstorm the ideas. All the proposals went back to the basic question: how to raise and lower boats quickly, while celebrating the joining of the two canals in a manner befitting the new Millennium.

The result was a wide variety of ideas from simple engineering structures to a purely aesthetic approach where the actual engineering was immersed within a larger artistic concept. Interestingly, the winning design looks to do both, combining art and engineering.

On the following pages, we look at six of the proposed (and rejected) alternatives – and then in some detail at the inspiration behind the favoured option: the organic spine consisting of a rotating sculptural beam which was conceived as an extension to the aqueduct.

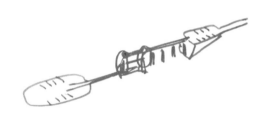

**Woodhorn – Experience Northumberland**

The Falkirk Wheel is a celebration that attempts to embrace the past, present and future. Other RMJM projects have aimed to achieve a similar impact.

Experience Northumberland is an existing museum and visitor centre at the redundant Woodhorn Colliery near Morpeth. This early proposal is to maximise the potential of the site by bringing the community archive onto the site and combining the museum and archive uses to create a new building type. The cutting edges of overlapping pickheads and of mechanical mining equipment are expressed in an extended and rotated roof form, which dramatically explodes out of the ground. This form comes from the radial layout of the archives surrounding a central reading room and museum gallery.

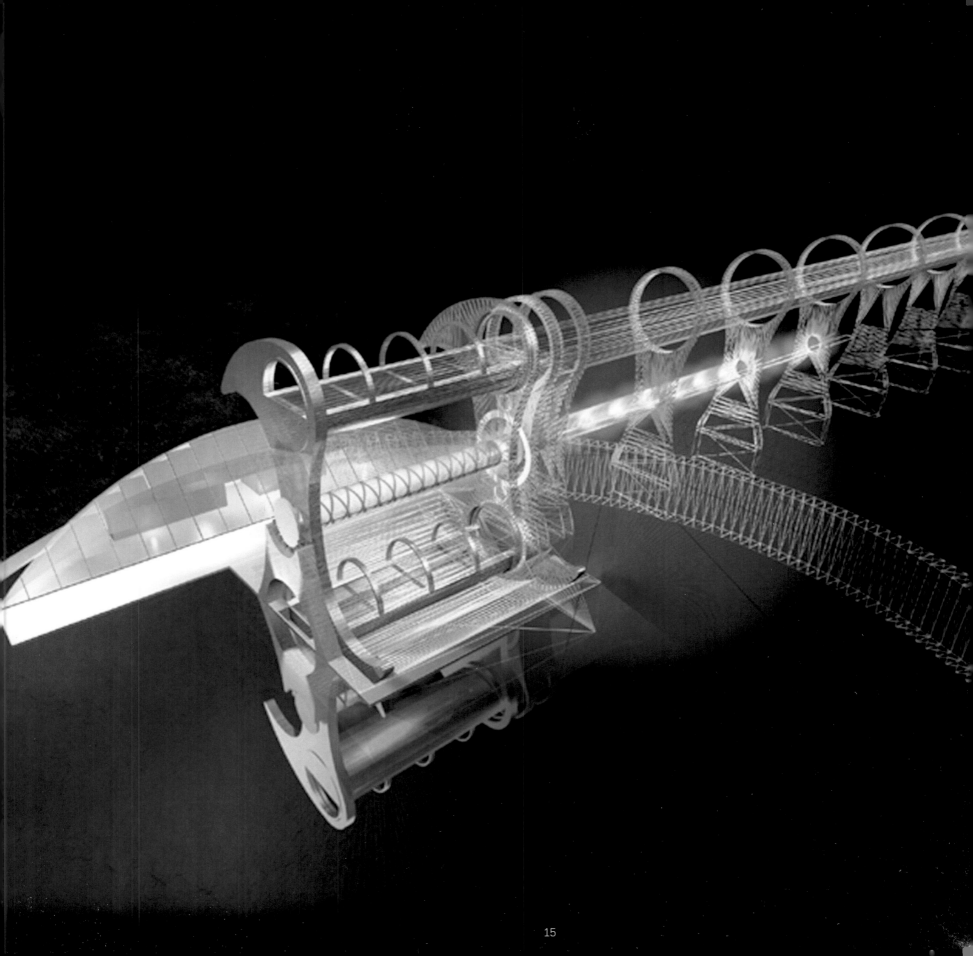

# The Balanced Lift

## Simple and pure, but not inspirational

The simplest of lifts uses the weight of one caisson to balance that of another in a similar way to a traditional elevator with lift car and counter weight. An additional drive motor is required but was never fully considered in this proposal. The suspended caissons would no doubt have resulted in a massively heavy support and guide structure compared to the sketch proposal.

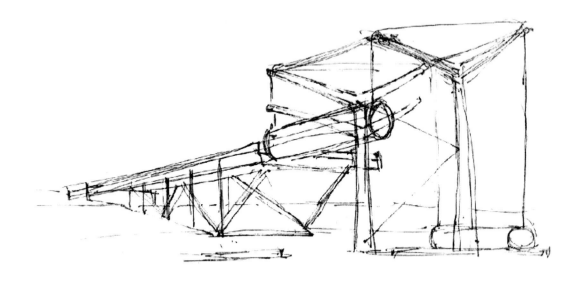

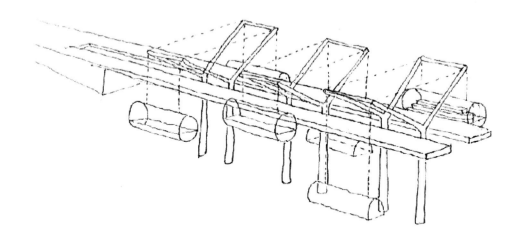

# The Counterweighted Circular Basin

Monumental flying saucer which would never be forgotten

This proposal was similar to the balanced lift, with counterweights surrounding a central moving basin. The horizontal loads on the cables would have required the supports to be much closer together than illustrated, but would have created a dramatic central form. The drive required to lift and lower the basin equally over 11 supports would have been a real mechanical engineering challenge.

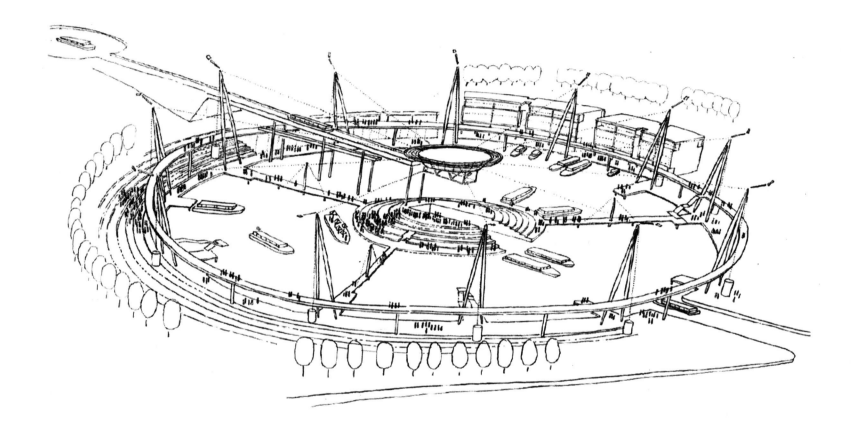

# The Rolling Egg

Mad but true! Enclosed within a steel egg in complete darkness

A rotating egg-shaped container half full of water allows boats to rise or fall in relation to the apparent width of the container. The container would have required to be almost entirely enclosed creating a memorable, but claustrophobic, experience.

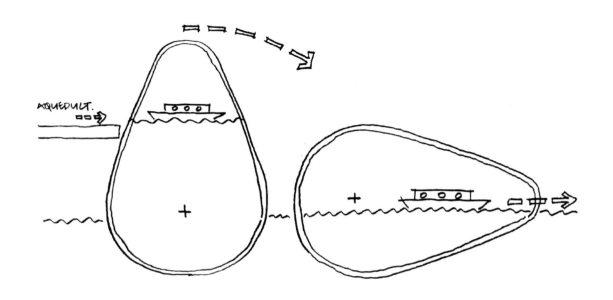

AQUEDULT.

# Inclined Plane/Spiral

Variations on the inclined plane to give more presence

The traditional inclined plane utilises a pair of railway bogies holding caissons, which in turn carry boats. The vertical loads are transferred to horizontal loads, which results in an efficient, if unremarkable, structure. The inclined spiral would have been a remarkable, but impossibly complex, variation.

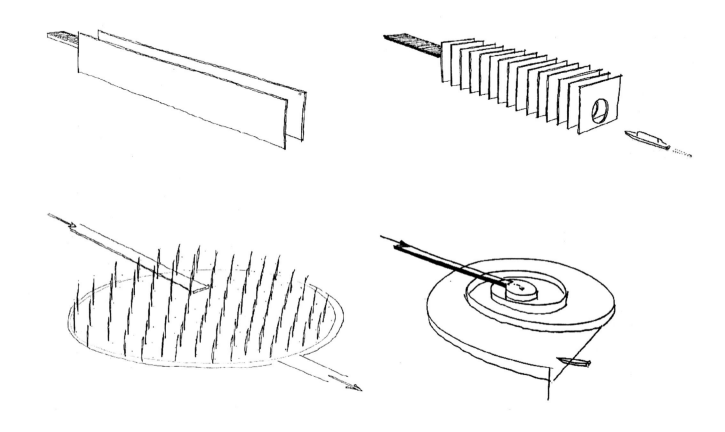

# The Wall of Water

A mystery lift hidden behind a wall of water

The lifting mechanism is hidden by a wall of water and becomes secondary to the spectacle of the aesthetic concept. However, this magician's trick may have been exposed by strong horizontal winds, which tend to prevail in this part of Scotland.

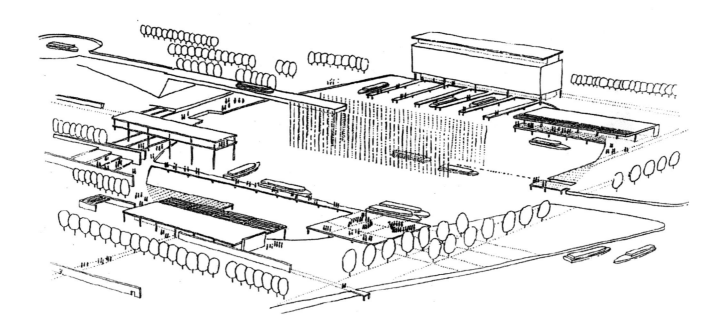

# The Oval Wheel

An elegant variation on the exemplar design with four caissons

This option offered an elegant variation on the exemplar design with four rotating caissons. What is magical about this is the mechanism required to maintain the horizontality of the caissons and the intersection of the ovular and circular forms.

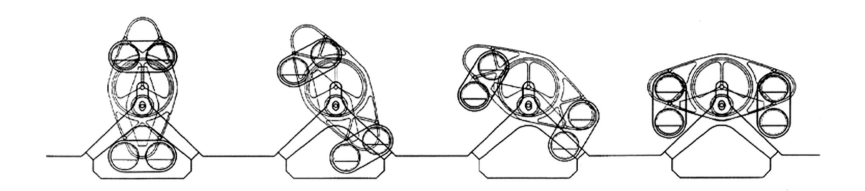

# The Organic Spine

A rotating sculptural beam conceived as an art work

The final solution for the Falkirk Wheel is ironically not a wheel, but a rotating beam. The structural and mechanical simplicity of the design had at its heart the idea of a linear organic form, or spine connecting the east and west coasts of Scotland. The organic form of the design is a symbolic structure which celebrates the joining of the two halves of Scotland, while also being expressive of movement and turning.

On the following pages, we look at some of the sources of inspiration that led to the winning RMJM design.

"There has been a definite attempt to design the Wheel for the 21st century. This design is considered to be a form of contemporary sculpture. The combination of the cultural and technical factors adds considerably to the effectiveness of the overall concept and has resulted in a truly exciting solution".

**The Royal Fine Art Commission for Scotland**

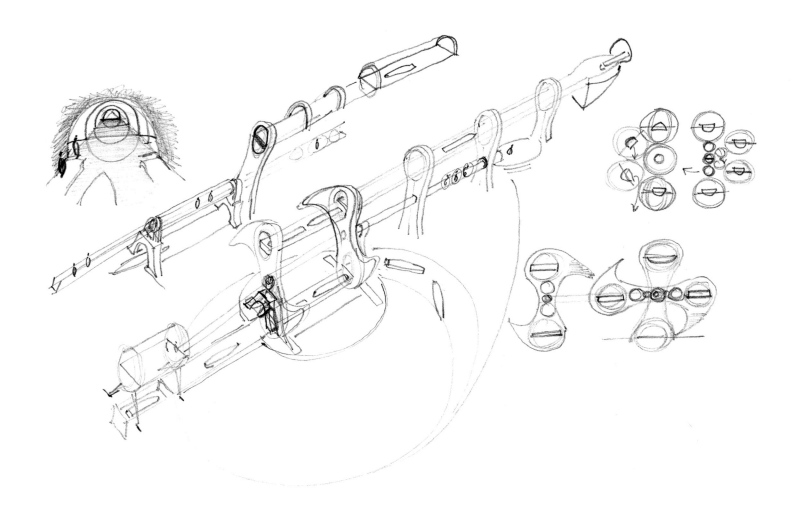

# From Ferris Wheel to Falkirk Wheel

As we have seen, the starting point in re-interpreting the wheel form was to re-invent the brief that had produced the previous proposals. The previous schemes had been developed on the simple idea of the wheel as a circle, as in a Ferris wheel. Our concept for the Wheel came out of the design for the aqueduct, which in turn grew out of the historical precedent of the stone aqueducts and viaducts built in the 18th and 19th centuries – and as far back as Roman times. These huge structures are beautiful objects. Their elegance arises from the repetition of simple forms defined by structural necessity and restricted by the availability of materials.

As this was a 'Millennium Project', we had to look to the future and aim to utilise the technology and materials that are available now to achieve forms that previously could not have been constructed.

We also looked to organic skeletal forms which have an inherent structural integrity and beauty. The spine of a fish skeleton provided the inspiration for the organic form of the aqueduct.

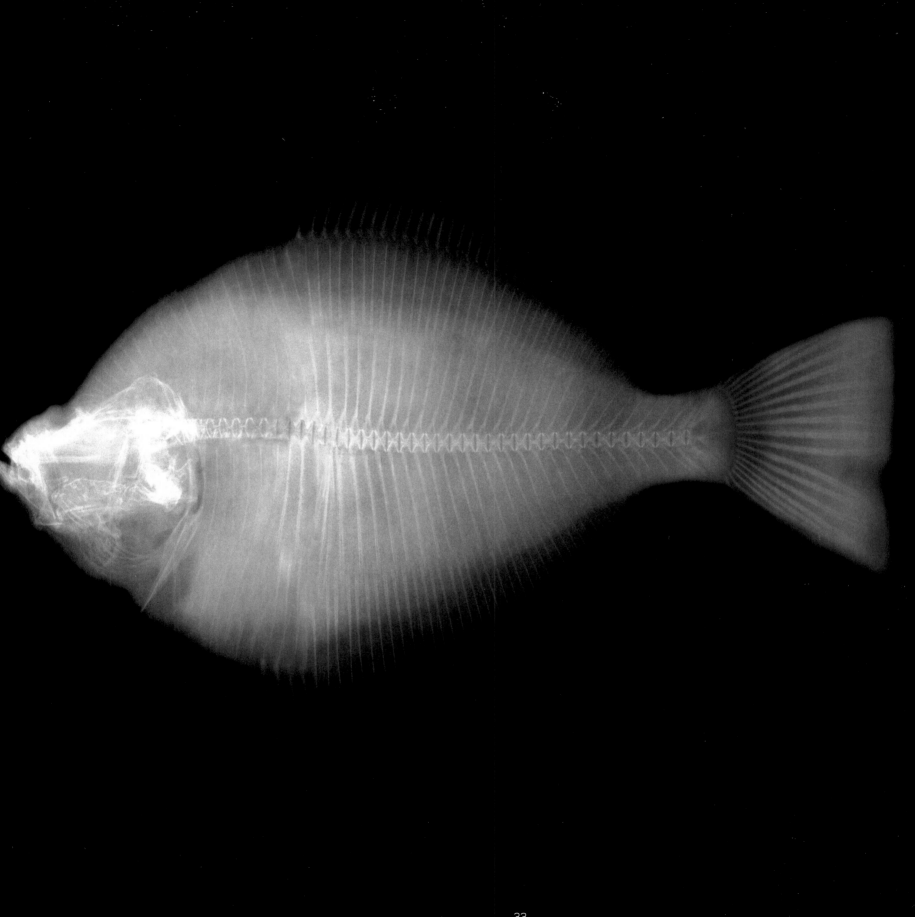

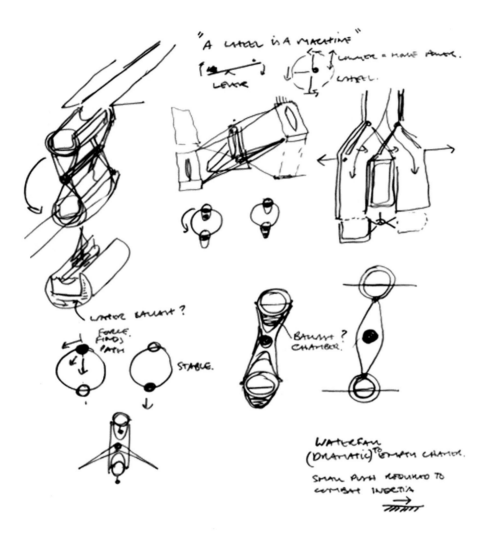

From the design for the aqueduct came the design for the Wheel. The aqueduct is the minimum width required to meet the client's brief for travelling on the canal. The Wheel therefore took the form of the aqueduct and developed it, adding direction by means of the hooked leading edges. This meant that rather than four caissons carrying one boat each, two caissons are used carrying two boats each. This simplified the structure of the wheel and allowed a dramatic reworking of the form of the structure.

There is an implicit beauty instilled
in linear repetitive objects such as
roads, canals, aqueducts or train
lines. In an architectural sense, this
is clearly seen in the New Town of
Edinburgh where the Georgian
architecture is repeated rigorously
to great effect. When the repeated
pattern is broken, it is to create a
dramatic entrance or a setting for a
public building. So it is for the Falkirk
Wheel, where the repeated static
form of the linear aqueduct is
broken by the hooked leading edges
which vividly express rotation
and movement.

# Innovation

## Engineering solutions

Having rejected the exemplar design in favour of a far simpler sculptural form of the Wheel, we had to ensure that the RMJM design was not compromised as the engineering and manufacturing constraints became more obvious throughout the design and build process.

This required a high degree of innovative thinking. For example, the hour glass figure of the arms was maintained despite initial concerns about the stresses concentrated around the central hub. Complex computer modelling illustrated how a slender form could work with 50mm thick steel.

To overcome this particular challenge and to find solutions to many others, RMJM continued to work closely with engineers from MG Bennet, Butterley Engineering and Arup – for the Wheel and Aqueduct respectively – throughout the design and construction period.

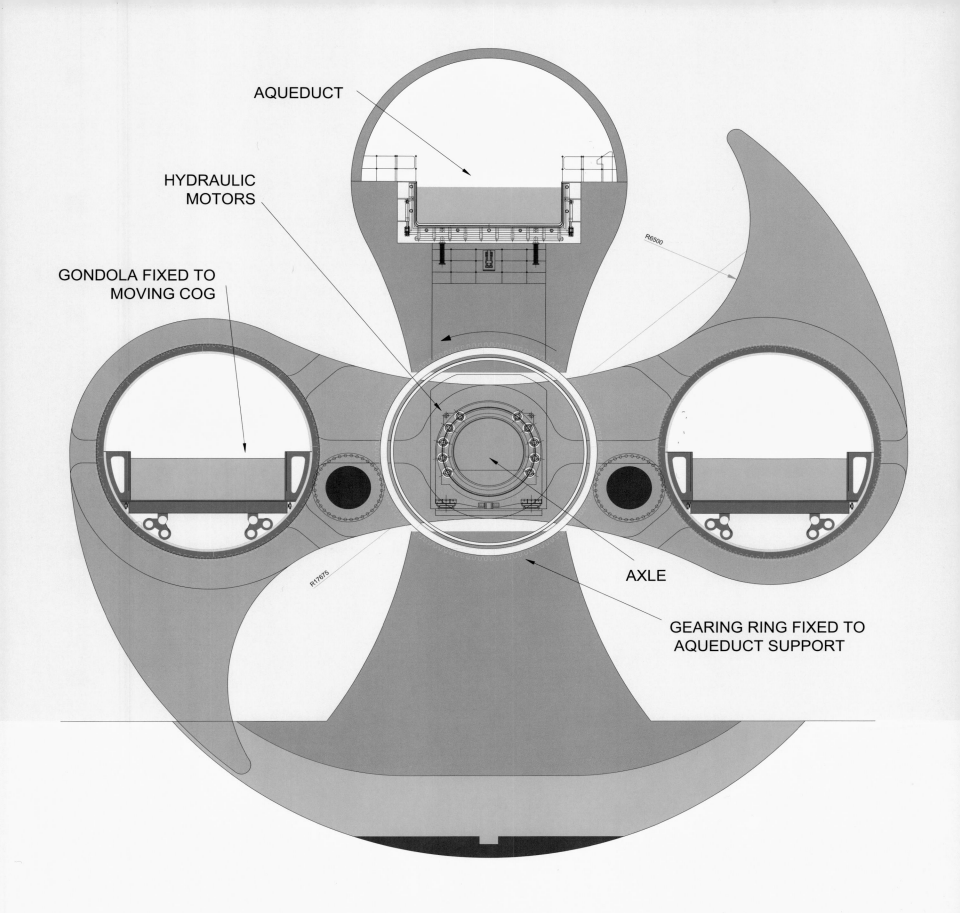

AQUEDUCT

HYDRAULIC
MOTORS

GONDOLA FIXED TO
MOVING COG

R6500

R17675

AXLE

GEARING RING FIXED TO
AQUEDUCT SUPPORT

# Innovation in action

As the project evolved, RMJM continued to play a key role – proposing solutions to a variety of engineering problems including the use of interlocking geared cogs to maintain the stability of the caissons that hold the boats as the Wheel turns.

The central cog is fixed in a static position around the central hub. Two smaller gears revolve around this as the Wheel turns, thus maintaining the horizontality of the final two gears which are attached to the end of the caissons. In this way the caissons cannot rock backwards and forwards and are positively located at all times.

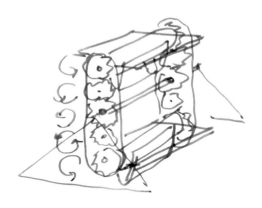

GRAVITY WHEEL.

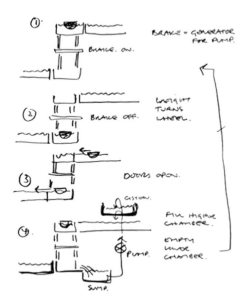

The concept for the gearing mechanism came out of the Wheel form where the circular caissons are enveloped by the hooked arms at each end which revolve around a central hub. With the help of a simple 'Lego' model, it soon became clear that the gears provided the simple solution to maintaining the stability of the caissons.

These gears do not, however, drive the arms of the Wheel, they are simply 'followers'. The actual drive mechanism consists of a series of eight hydraulic motors mounted in the last aqueduct support, which require a tiny amount of electrical power to turn. The structure is incredibly quiet as it revolves and takes on a different quality whether moving or stationary, reflected in the water of the basin in which it sits.

The aqueduct was originally developed as a series of re-inforced concrete piers, standing 25 metres apart with a circular opening at the head of each pier to hold a semi-circular re-inforced concrete aqueduct.

Subsequently, this design evolved due the practicalities of accommodating the full boat depth across the entire breadth of the aqueduct, giving the flat base that now exists. This development also created the moon-shaped opening between the head of the supports and the underside of the aqueduct – a detail which purposely allows the aqueduct to be seen as one continuous element which visually floats over the supports.

Other modifications to the original design for the aqueduct were unavoidable due to cost constraints. For example, the hub had initially been illustrated as a glass-wrapped helix type structure which would have allowed unparalleled views for the spectator of the Wheel moving around it. This was lost due to the cost of the structure and the need to drive both arms of the Wheel from the rear support. Initially the Wheel was to be driven from both the front and rear supports by independent hydraulic motors, but a more cost effective solution was to drive the arms from the rear support with a solid central hub acting as a drive shaft for the front arms.

# From design to build

Following receipt of statutory approvals, the detailed design of the Wheel progressed and the general form remained as per the concept described earlier. However, we continued to face new engineering challenges that threatened to compromise our vision.

One particular problem was encountered in accommodating the movement of the aqueduct structure, while providing a waterproof seal at the Wheel connection. This resulted, for a short period, in the deletion of the moon-shaped openings at the head of the supports. However, Arup, the structural engineers for the aqueduct and design co-ordinators for the project, developed an alternative detail where a special section of steel aqueduct is located at the joint between the aqueduct and the Wheel, thus accommodating all movement while taking account of the tolerances required to provide a waterproof seal.

Other changes arose through the design and build process as pressures inevitably mounted on cost. Some may arguably have impacted on the quality of the finished product, but others are part of the functional make-up of a major piece of civil engineering and actually add to the robust quality of the design.

The Wheel itself was manufactured in the workshops of Butterley Engineering in Derby. Butterley specialise in constructing massive cranes and heavy engineering for ship yards, docks or mining and have used their experience to integrate tried and tested technologies into the engineering of the Wheel.

Even so, the rotation of the Wheel created a complex problem for the engineers as the individual elements move from tension to compression, quite unlike anything that Butterleys had constructed previously. Indeed, as the Wheel turns, most of the steel elements face repeated 100 per cent stress reversals as they alternate between tension and compression.

Due to the individual curved form of the Wheel, the fabrication work was carried out by hand by skilled craftsmen who used specialist equipment to carve the huge pieces of steel to the correct profile based on extremely accurate steel templates. The whole construction was assembled in the workshop to check the fit prior to transport to the construction site. Due to transport restrictions, the arms were transported in sections and bolted together on site prior to erection.

In all there were 12 pieces to make up the curved box beam arms, a three-part axle and multi-section gondolas. The steel thickness ranges from 10mm to 50mm depending on the stresses involved. Fifteen thousand bolts were required with 45,000 boltholes drilled into the steel sections and flange plates.

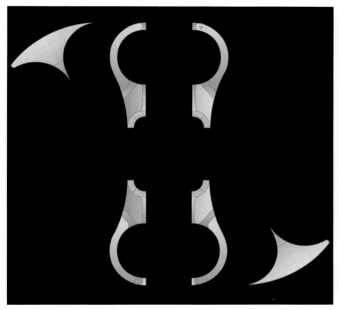
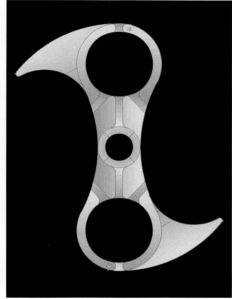

# Revelation

## The sense of arrival

The sense of arrival that people experience as they approach the Wheel was considered from the perspective of all users and visitors from day one. In particular, we considered the point of view of the boat users approaching the Wheel from the Forth and Clyde Canal to the north and the Union Canal to the south.

These approaches are obviously very different with one coming from above and one below, one to the rear and one to the front face. In both approaches there is a sequence of events that extends the arrival zone and increases the excitement and theatre of the boat lift.

"Lord Dalkeith, a millennium commissioner, has described the Wheel as "a wonderful new icon for Scotland, a lasting legacy". It is already on the way to attaining iconic status. Future generations will pass judgement on whether it is a lasting legacy. It certainly deserves to be. The Wheel is not only a physical link. It is a symbolic link between Scotland's past and its future."

**The Herald, 25 May 2002**

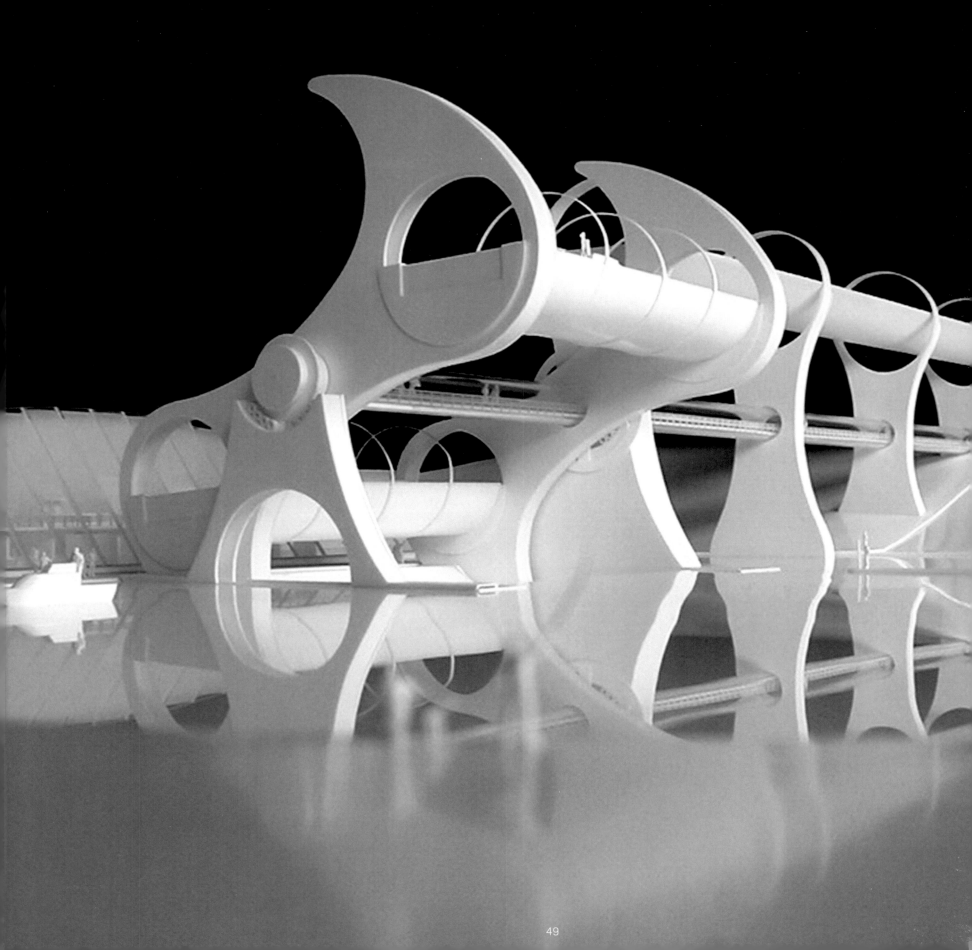

From the Union Canal, the approach is prefaced by a series of historical locks that raise the boat to above the level of the aqueduct. At the termination of the historical canal route the canal drops sharply, widens and turns to the right to provide a waiting area at the mouth of a tunnel. This is the tunnel that takes the Millennium Link underneath the Antonine Wall, a historic monument which marks the Roman Empire's deepest advance into Scotland. It is somehow fitting, therefore, that the new aqueduct with its echoes of Roman engineering should follow directly from this tunnel, but in an uncompromisingly contemporary form. The tunnel entrance is as tight as it can be to allow a single boat along the 100 metre long tunnel.

Before boats exit the tunnel, the view ahead is framed by the semi-circular silhouette of the tunnel mouth. This semi-circle shape is repeated in the hoops that form the head of the aqueduct supports. Together they define the termination of the aqueduct and the connection to the Wheel. The Wheel itself replicates the geometry of the aqueduct exactly and the only clue to the fact that it turns are the hooked leading edges. At the end of the aqueduct, the view ahead to the Campsie Fells and beyond is framed by a semi-circular opening reminiscent of the Japanese marumado, or circular window.

The edge of the caisson where the water ends appears incredibly thin, marked only by the 200mm thick folding gate which opens to allow boats to exit when the Wheel has performed a half rotation. Of course, the visual thinness of the edge underplays the reality of the robust engineering. However, anyone who has ever crewed a canal boat will recall the momentum a boat has even when moving at slow speed. So approaching such an apparently thin edge, some 35 metres above the ground, can be an interesting experience!

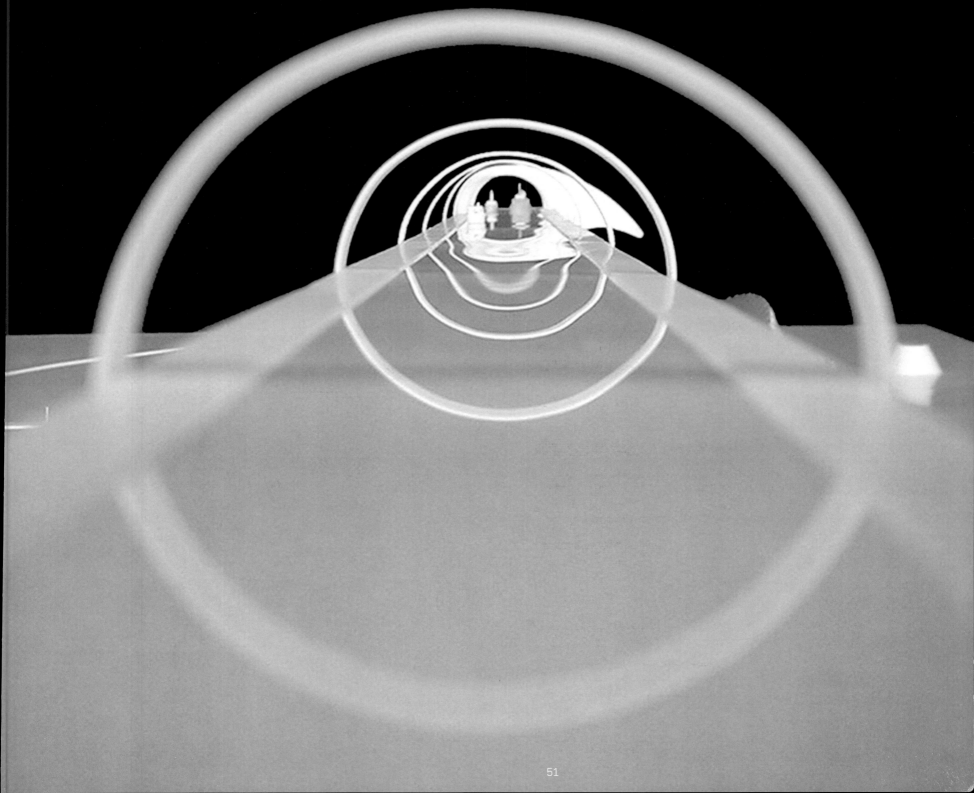

Once the boat enters the caisson there is a short delay while the gates close behind it. The Wheel then begins to turn slowly towards the visitor centre, gliding almost without sound on the rails which encircle the caissons.

For a short moment, as the Wheel moves horizontally, the semi-circular openings at the end of the aqueduct and the caisson become separated and the view is split into two parts.

The movement of the Wheel horizontally pushes the caisson over towards the visitor centre with no apparent means of support. Then, almost above the building, the caisson begins to move dramatically downwards. As it nears the boardwalk below it moves back onto its original alignment, closely missing the spectators below. This movement, combined with the hooked arms, produces an ever-changing panorama of intersecting curves.

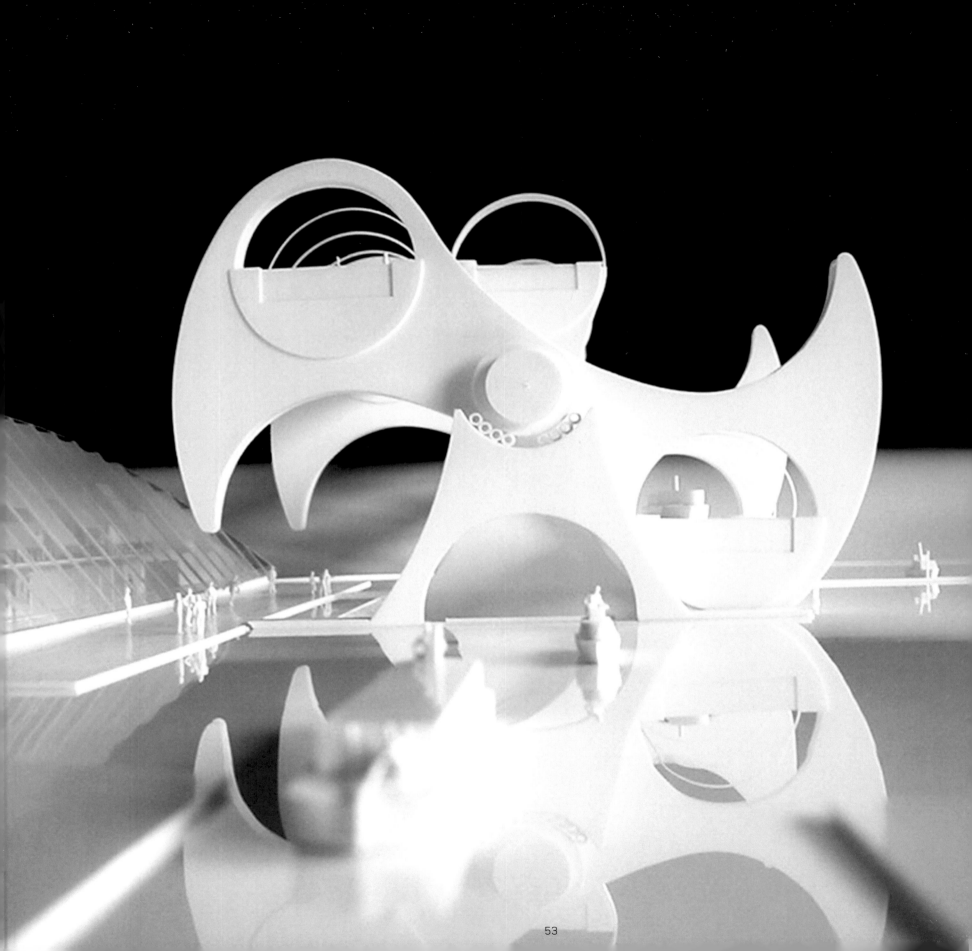

The approach by road was determined by the limited access. This created a difficult problem, which was solved by the positioning of the visitor centre almost as a screen to restrict the view and increase the sense of anticipation.

As a result, the visitor sees the Wheel from afar as a monumental structure. On moving closer, it disappears from view behind the visitor centre and then reappears only when it is towering above. The car park is located slightly back from the visitor centre, ensuring the same effect is repeated as visitors walk from the car park to the main entrance.

The approach by boat from the Forth and Clyde Canal begins with glimpses of the structure in the distance seen through a veil of trees. As the boat comes closer to the basin, the Wheel disappears from sight and the lock gates open to allow access into the basin lock. The lock gates close and the water enters the lock chamber, slowly raising the boat and allowing the view of the Wheel to be exposed. The lock provides a dramatic entrance to the basin on a direct axis to the Wheel. Part of the reasoning for the lock is to allow the basin to be drained when required, but it also has the benefit of providing this grand entrance to the basin. Once in the basin, boats can move around the circular form and moor alongside the visitor centre.

From the basin, boats move into the caisson through a semi-circular archway which supports the massive structure of the Wheel above. The gates then close and the boat is lifted upwards away from the visitor centre. There is no obvious drive mechanism for either the Wheel turning or for the movement of the caissons within the arms. There is only the feeling of being effortlessly lifted. As the Wheel rises, it begins to make its way back towards the aqueduct support and the two semi-circular apertures slowly align to reveal a vista leading through the hoops of the aqueduct towards the tunnel mouth beyond.

For any visitor walking out from the visitor centre underneath the slowly turning hooks, it can seem that they are coming down directly overhead. As the hooks approach the boardwalk, however, their curved form takes them naturally away from the spectator and allows them to disappear safely into the ground.

The organic form and the huge mass, combined with the slow speed of the movement, gives the Wheel an almost animalistic character – similar to that of a friendly herbaceous dinosaur!

"This is a creation which is opportunistically placed to take advantage of topography. It is not cowed by the rampart of the Antonine Wall beside it. Viewed from the north across fields and straggling suburbs it is a moving sight: an enormous installation in the form of an avian profile; of a forgotten mark abandoned by a race of giant proof-readers; a piece of swarf from one of Falkirk's scrapyards cleaned inflated a thousandfold"

**Jonathan Meades, The Times, 10 August 2002**

# Exploration

## Art and engineering

The Falkirk Wheel is the answer to a problem that need not have existed but for the arrogance of the 1960s when the canal network across central Scotland was ruined. To join the canals together once more was a challenge that could have had many physical forms, but a pure piece of engineering would have answered only the functional questions asked of it and would have missed the opportunity to create something far more intriguing and exciting.

Within RMJM, the project to design the Wheel was always seen as something symbolic. Something that would combine both art and engineering. Something that would ask questions of the culture and the people who created it. Something that would encourage people in central Scotland – and beyond – to explore ideas about where we come from, where we are now and where we might yet go.

We always intended then that the Wheel should be more than a piece of functional engineering – and in this section we begin to explore the landscape of art and engineering to discover where the Wheel may lie on a line drawn between these two poles.

# Exhibit A.

On a hill overlooking the approach to Newcastle, the 'Angel of the North' stands proud; a monument to the industry and skills of an age gone by, where heavy industry and the shipyards kept the north-east alive.

This is one of a series of sculptures by Anthony Gormley in which he explores his inner self through the adaptation of his own body in sculptural forms. It is interesting that the angel faces south towards the political centre of Britain. It could have faced north or east towards the sea. Would the message it sends out have been different then? If it did turn its head northwards now it would see how commercial and retail activity has replaced the historic heavy industry of the Tyne valley.

# Exhibit B.

A 'flock' of wind-powered generators
dominate a Highland hillside. These
massive revolving landmarks are the
unmistakable marks of progress for
many – clean power, clean lines. They
are unashamedly functional objects
but they have an intrinsic beauty
due to their aerodynamic form.
Propellers are beautiful, functional
objects. They are complete in
themselves, but also dynamic and full
of movement.  It is perhaps fitting
that they appear in groups, rather
than as individual objects, almost as
an expression of their mass-
produced origin.

# Connections and divisions

In Central Scotland, the traditional industries have been similar to those of north-east England – so it is not surprising that there is a similar generosity of spirit and a similar need to celebrate the achievements of the past, even while looking forward.

The leisure and tourism industry is now a major earner for Scotland and the repair of the canal network will surely be a key part of revenue generation in the central belt. However, the prosperity of the central belt remains firmly divided between Edinburgh and Glasgow – two great cities with a tendency to ignore each other and the rest of Scotland.

It was interesting that the debate on the location of the Scottish Parliament clearly showed this division between the two cities. It is also clear that the concept which underpins the winning design for the new Parliament is to create something 'of the land'; something for Scotland, rather than for Edinburgh alone; something that makes connections and overcomes divisions.

"We do not see the built environment as a priority.  When new buildings go up we do not seem to rate them.  Take the carping about the cost of the Scottish Parliament at Holyrood. Yes, it is expensive and the cost was underestimated, but it is likely to become a building that not only defines Scotland, but also helps its economy by the tourists it attracts.  The same could be said of the Falkirk Wheel.  People will marvel at the structure, but they will also be able to use it.  It will be a living landmark with a cultural impact that is valuable and long-term."

**The Herald, 25 May 2002**

# Imagination

## Images and insights

So in the same way as the new Scottish Parliament – another RMJM project – sets out to make a statement about the nation, what is it that the Falkirk Wheel has to say about Scotland? What connections does it make? What divisions does it try to overcome? Why is it art and engineering?

Well, in part it sets out to celebrate the industrial achievements of the past in the same way that the 'angel' does for the north-east of England. However, the Wheel is also a singular piece of innovative engineering – one which is incredibly simple but, unlike the understated minimalism of windmills, it is also one which presents a passionate riot of elegant curves.

And this is intentional. To celebrate something of the magnitude of the Millennium Link, we had to invest the functional structure with an energy well beyond that of 'the ordinary'. We had to aim to give it the drama and theatre that is required to put it on an international stage. This act of celebration is what gives the Wheel its radical form.

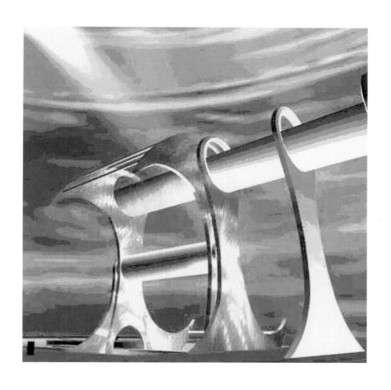

And its radical form is also a reflection of its geographical location. Naturally, the physical location of the Wheel was limited by the availability of land and so it has to sit in a natural basin – almost lost from view except for glimpses from distant hills.

As a result, a less powerful structure would have been buried in this agricultural landscape. It would have risked being completely obliterated and absorbed. As it is, however, the Wheel appears to lift its head to take stock of its Scottish surroundings. It stands up proud and bold, emerging from the land as the skeletal frame of a long lost prehistoric animal.

"Modern architecture is not all bad. Structures such as the Wheel and the science centre in Glasgow make a huge contribution to culture. Modern buildings should not just be for prestige. They are at their best and most imposing when they enrich us and our cultural tapestry. The Wheel has huge potential to do both."

**The Herald, 25 May 2002**

The skeletal form is again no accident. One of the main inspirations behind the design concept was that of the spine of a fish, a beautiful linear object made up of a series of repetitive organic elements such as the piers of the aqueduct.

Yet this is also a spine that connects the east and west coasts of Scotland. If the Wheel is symbolic of joining, it is perhaps the buckle on the central belt of Scotland. It says Scotland is whole once more. Ying and yang are joined to create harmony.

In that sense, and taking into account the innovative engineering which hints at a revival of the entrepreneurial spirit, the Falkirk Wheel reverberates with the strength and passion, the vision and imagination that have underpinned the very best of Scottish culture since the 18th century Enlightenment and, more importantly, it stands as one monument – celebrating not just the past, but what may be possible in the future if Scotland's two major cities, now symbolically reunited by the Wheel, were to work together towards common goals.

# Gallery

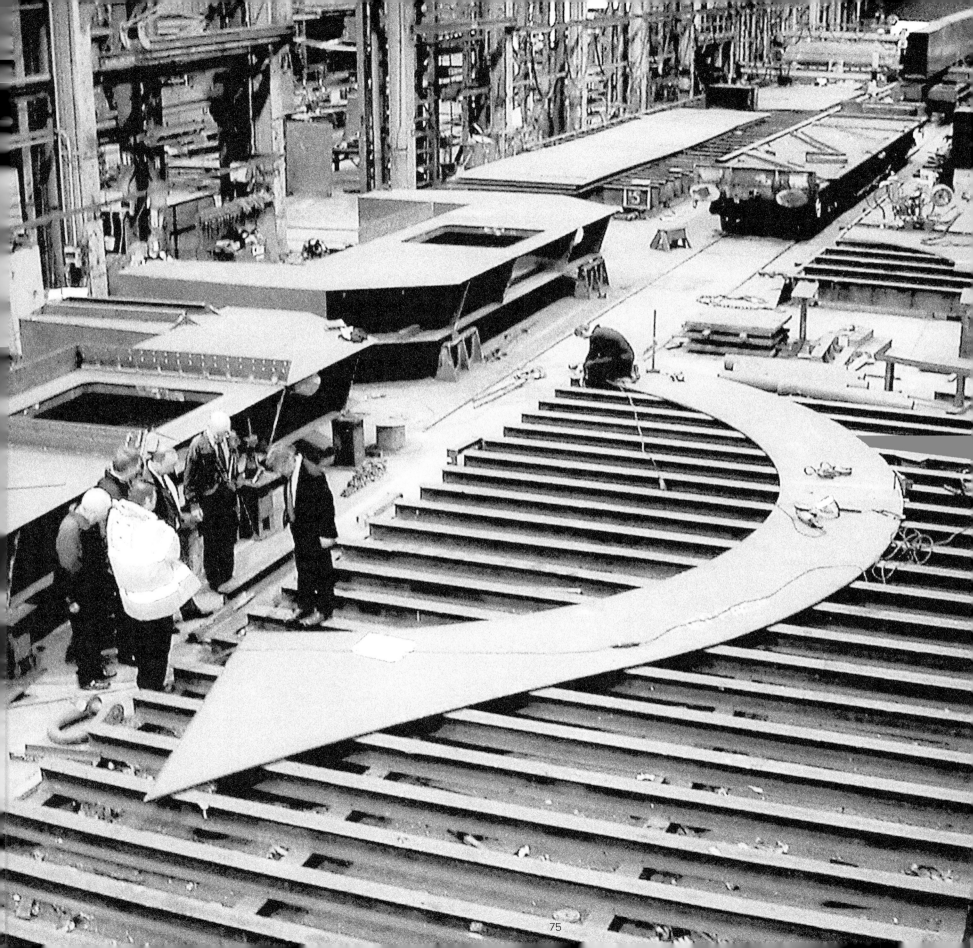

KEEP CLEAR
OF OPEN DOOR

94

S 8 DOUBLE DECKER BUSES ↘ UP TO 8 BOATS · 35M WIDE · LOADS AS HEAVY AS 177 ELEPHANTS

IRK WHEEL WORK?

WATER GO UPHILL?

ILT?

Y HAVE A WHEEL?

A trade route across Scotland

the origin

EDINBURGH

# Collaboration

## Roles and responsibilities

**Project Team**

| | |
|---|---|
| Client: | British Waterways Scotland |
| | Jim Stirling |
| | George Ballinger |
| | Marischal Ellis |
| Architect: | RMJM |
| | Tony Kettle, Falkirk Wheel |
| | Paul Stallan, Master Planning and Visitor Centre |
| Main contractor: | Morrison-Bachy Solentanche JV |
| | Jim Steele |
| | Bernie Keirnan |
| Civil Engineering Consultant (Aqueduct): | Arup |
| | Alan Richmond |
| | Oliver Riches |
| Wheel Supplier (Structural Design Fabrication, Erection): | Butterley Ltd |
| | Colin Castledine |
| | Julian Bonfield |
| Structural and Mechanical Engineering Sub-consultant, Mechanical Engineering design and co-ordination | MG Bennet and Associates |
| | Nick Cooper |
| Detailed Structural Engineering Sub-consultant: | Tony Gee & Partners |
| | Richard Prosser |

# Tony Kettle

## BA Arch (Hons) DipArch RIBA ARIAS

Tony Kettle joined RMJM Scotland Ltd in 1989 and was appointed Director of RMJM in 1997. He is currently Director for Europe and the Middle East, and was responsible for the Falkirk Wheel.

Tony was born in 1965 near Whitley Bay, Newcastle, and has lived in Scotland since 1973. He was educated at Edinburgh College of Art and Heriot-Watt University between 1982 and 1988. He is married to Denise, and has three children, the eldest of which is Sarah, whose Lego he famously borrowed to demonstrate his innovative gearing mechanism for keeping the Wheel's caissons horizontal!

As an RMJM director, Tony has been involved in a wide range of projects from museums to office buildings and hotels including the Hermitage Museum in St Petersburg, The Scottish Office in Leith, the Dubai World Trade Centre in UAE and the Scottish Parliament in Edinburgh. Smaller projects include exhibition and furniture design, bespoke lighting design and street furniture.

Key projects in 2002 include Doncaster Racecourse, Doncaster Education City, Woodhorn Colliery Museum (Experience Northumberland), Palm Island in Dubai and the Music and Performing Arts College in Newcastle.

Tony's approach to projects is collaborative, generated from working within a stimulating multi-skill environment including architects, engineers and other design professionals. He is interested in the role of art in extending the boundaries of architecture, engineering and landscape design.

**Funding**

Funding for the £78m Millennium Link was led by a £32.2m grant from the Millennium Commission, £18.7m from Scottish Enterprise and £8.6m from the European Union, with £9.3m from British Waterways, £7m raised by seven local councils and £2.4m from the private sector.

**Awards**

Structural Steel Design Award 2002

Institute of Civil Engineers 'Brunel Medal' 2002

Nominated for BCIA Award 2002

Winner of the Saltire Award 2002

**Contact**

For further information please contact Tony Kettle, **tk@rmjm.com**

**RMJM**

10 Bells Brae

Edinburgh

EH4 3BJ